I0494025

Occupational Safety and Health Act of 1970

"To assure safe and healthful working conditions for working men and women; by authorizing enforcement of the standards developed under the Act; by assisting and encouraging the States in their efforts to assure safe and healthful working conditions; by providing for research, information, education, and training in the field of occupational safety and health..."

This informational booklet is intended to provide an overview of frequently used OSHA standards in the Construction industry. This publication does not itself alter or determine compliance responsibilities, which are set forth in OSHA standards themselves and the *Occupational Safety and Health Act*.

Employers and employees in the 27 states and territories that operate their own OSHA-approved workplace safety and health plans should check with their state safety and health agency. Their state may be enforcing standards and other procedures that, while "at least as effective as" federal standards, are not always identical to the federal requirements. For more information on states with OSHA-approved state plans, please visit: http://www. osha.gov/dcsp/osp/index.html

Material contained in this publication is in the public domain and may be reproduced, fully or partially, without permission. Source credit is requested but not required.

This information will be made available to sensory-impaired individuals upon request. Voice phone: (202) 693-1999; teletypewriter (TTY) number: 1-877-889-5627.

Construction Industry Digest

U.S. Department of Labor

Occupational Safety and Health Administration

OSHA 2202-09
2011 (Revised)

U.S. Department of Labor
Hilda L. Solis, Secretary of Labor

Contents

Foreword

The Construction Industry Digest contains summaries of the most frequently used standards in the construction industry. The standards are presented alphabetically followed by the reference to the appropriate regulation. With few exceptions, standards in this digest are from *Title 29 of the Code of Federal Regulations (CFR)*, Part 1926.

Remember, this booklet is only a digest of basic applicable standards and should not be considered as a complete substitute for any provisions of the *Occupational Safety and Health Act of 1970* (OSH Act), or for any standards issued under the OSH Act. The requirements discussed in this publication are summarized and abbreviated. The actual source standards are referenced at the end of each topic discussed; consult the CFR for a more complete explanation of the specific standards listed.

General

Employers have the responsibility to provide a safe workplace. **Employers MUST provide their employees with a workplace that does not have serious hazards and follow all relevant OSHA safety and health standards.**

Employers must comply with specific standards. All employers in the construction industry must also have injury and illness prevention programs. Contractors and employers who do construction work must comply with standards in 29 CFR 1926. Subpart C, *General Safety and Health Provisions*, as well as other specific sections of these standards, include the responsibilities for each contractor/employer to initiate and maintain injury and illness prevention programs, provide for a competent person to conduct frequent and regular inspections, and instruct each employee to recognize and avoid unsafe conditions and know what regulations are applicable to the work environment. Employees must be provided training in a language and vocabulary they can understand.

OSHA Worksite Investigations

OSHA conducts on-site inspections of worksites to enforce the OSHA law that protects workers and their rights. Inspections are initiated without advance notice, conducted using on-site or telephone and facsimile investigations, and performed by highly trained compliance officers. Worksite inspections are conducted based on the following priorities:

- Imminent danger;
- A fatality or hospitalizations;
- Worker complaints and referrals;
- Targeted inspections – particular hazards, high injury rates; and
- Follow-up inspections.

Inspections are conducted without employers knowing when or where they will occur. The employer is not informed in advance that there will be an inspection, regardless of whether it is in response to a complaint or is a programmed inspection.

Frequently Used Standards in Construction

Access to Medical and Exposure Records

Each employer shall permit employees, their designated representatives, and OSHA direct access to employer-maintained exposure and medical records. The standard limits access only to those employees who are, have been (including former employees), or will be exposed to toxic substances or harmful physical agents. **1910.1020 made applicable to construction by 1926.33**

Each employer must preserve and maintain accurate medical and exposure records for each employee. Exposure records and data analyses based on them are to be kept for 30 years. Medical records are to be kept for at least the duration of employment plus 30 years. Background data for exposure records such as laboratory reports and work sheets need to be kept for only 1 year. **1910.1020(b)(3), .1020(d)(1)(i), and .1020(d)(1)(ii)**

Records of employees who have worked for less than 1 year need not be retained after employment if they are provided to the employee upon the termination of employment. First-aid records of one-time treatment need not be retained for any specified period. **1910.1020(d)(1)(i) (B) and (C)**

Aerial Lifts

Aerial lifts, powered or manual, include, but are not limited to, the following types of vehicle-mounted aerial devices used to elevate personnel to jobsites above ground: extensible boom platforms, aerial ladders, articulating boom platforms, and vertical towers. **1926.453(a)(1)**

When operating aerial lifts, employers must ensure that employees are

- Trained,
- Authorized,
- Setting brakes,
- Positioning outriggers on pads or a solid surface,
- Not exceeding boom and basket load limits,
- Attached to the boom or basket with a restraint device or personal fall arrest system,
- Standing firmly on the floor of the basket,
- Not climbing on the edge of the basket or using ladders, planks, or other devices for a work position. **1926.453(b) and 1926.454**

In addition, manufacturers (or the equivalent, such as a nationally recognized testing laboratory) must certify in writing that all modifications to aerial lifts conform to applicable OSHA and ANSI A92.2-1969 provisions, and are at least as safe as the equipment was before modification. **1926.453(a)(2)**

Air Tools

Pneumatic power tools shall be secured to the hose in a positive manner to prevent accidental disconnection. **1926.302(b)(1)**

Safety clips or retainers shall be securely installed and maintained on pneumatic impact tools to prevent attachments from being accidentally expelled. **1926.302(b)(2)**

The manufacturer's safe operating pressure for all fittings shall not be exceeded. **1926.302(b)(5)**

All hoses exceeding 1/2-inch (1.3-centimeters) inside diameter shall have a safety device at the source of supply or branch line to reduce pressure in case of hose failure. **1926.302(b)(7)**

Asbestos

Each employer who has a workplace or work operation where exposure monitoring is required must perform monitoring to determine accurately the airborne concentrations of asbestos to which employees may be exposed. **1926.1101(f)(1)(i)**

Employers also must ensure that no employee is exposed to an airborne concentration of asbestos in excess of 0.1 fiber per cubic centimeter of air (f/cc) as an 8-hour time-weighted average (TWA). **1926.1101(c)(1)**

In addition, employers must ensure that no employee is exposed to an airborne concentration of asbestos in excess of 1 f/cc as averaged over a sampling period of 30 minutes. **1926.1101(c)(2)**

Respirators must be used during (1) all Class I asbestos jobs; (2) all Class II work where an asbestos-containing material is not removed substantially intact; (3) all Class II and III work not using wet methods, except on sloped roofs; (4) all Class II and III work without a negative exposure assessment; (5) all Class III jobs where thermal system insulation or surfacing asbestos-containing or presumed asbestos-containing material is cut, abraded, or broken; (6) all Class IV work within a regulated area where respirators are required; (7) all work where employees are exposed above the PEL or STEL; and (8) in emergencies. **1926.1101(h)(1)(i) through (viii)**.

The employer must provide and require the use of protective clothing – such as coveralls or similar whole-body clothing, head coverings, gloves, and foot coverings – for

- Any employee exposed to airborne asbestos exceeding the PEL or STEL,
- Work without a negative exposure assessment, or
- Any employee performing Class I work involving the removal of over 25 linear or 10 square feet (10 square meters) of thermal system insulation or surfacing asbestos containing or presumed asbestos-containing materials. **1926.1101(i)(1)**

The employer must provide a medical surveillance program for all employees who – for a combined total of 30 or more days per year – engage in Class I, II, or III work or are exposed at or above the PEL or STEL; or who wear negative-pressure respirators. **1926.1101(m)(1)(i)**

Belt Sanding Machines

Belt sanding machines shall be provided with guards at each nip point where the sanding belt runs onto a pulley. **1926.304(f), incorporated from ANSI 01.1-1961, Section 4.9.4**

The unused run of the sanding belt shall be guarded against accidental contact. **1926.304(f), incorporated from ANSI 01.1-1961, Section 4.9.4**

Chains (See Wire Ropes, Chains, and Ropes)

Chemicals (See Gases, Vapors, Fumes, Dusts, and Mists; Asbestos; Lead; Silica; and Hazard Communication)

Compressed Air, Use of

Compressed air used for cleaning purposes shall be reduced to less than 30 pounds per square inch (psi) and then only with effective chip guarding and personal protective equipment. This requirement does not apply to concrete form, mill scale, and similar cleaning operations. **1926.302(b)(4)**

Compressed Gas Cylinders

Valve protection caps shall be in place and secured when compressed gas cylinders are transported, moved, or stored. **1926.350(a)(1)**

Cylinder valves shall be closed when work is finished and when cylinders are empty or are moved. **1926.350(a)(8)**

Compressed gas cylinders shall be secured in an upright position at all times, except if necessary for short periods of time when cylinders are actually being hoisted or carried. **1926.350(a)(9)**

Cylinders shall be kept far enough away from the actual welding or cutting operations so that sparks, hot slag, or flame will not reach them. When this is impractical, fire-resistant shields shall be provided. Cylinders shall be placed where they cannot become part of an electrical circuit. **1926.350(b)(1) through (2)**

Oxygen and fuel gas pressure regulators, including their related gauges, shall be in proper working order while in use. **1926.350(h)**

Concrete and Masonry Construction

No construction loads shall be placed on a concrete structure or portion of a concrete structure unless the employer determines, based on information received from a person who is qualified in structural design, that the structure or portion of the structure is capable of supporting the loads. **1926.701(a)**

No employee shall be permitted to work under concrete buckets while buckets are being elevated or lowered into position. **1926.701(e)(1)**

To the extent practical, elevated concrete buckets shall be routed so that no employee or the fewest number of employees is exposed to the hazards associated with falling concrete buckets. **1926.701(e)(2)**

Formwork shall be designed, fabricated, erected, supported, braced, and maintained so that it is capable of supporting – without failure – all vertical and lateral loads that may reasonably be anticipated to be applied to the formwork. **1926.703(a)(1)**

Forms and shores (except those used for slabs on grade and slip forms) shall not be removed until the employer determines that the concrete has gained sufficient strength to support its weight and superimposed loads. Such determination shall be based on compliance with one of the following:

- The plans and specifications stipulate conditions for removal of forms and shores, and such conditions have been followed, or
- The concrete has been properly tested with an appropriate American Society for Testing Materials (ASTM) standard test method designed to indicate the concrete compressive strength, and the test results indicate that the concrete has gained sufficient strength to support its weight and superimposed loads. (ASTM, 100 Barr Harbor Drive, West Conshohocken, PA 19428; (610) 832-9585). **1926.703(e)(1)(i) through (ii)**

A limited access zone shall be established whenever a masonry wall is being constructed. The limited access zone shall conform to the following:

- Established prior to the start of construction of the wall,
- Equal to the height of the wall to be constructed plus 4 feet (1.2 meters), and shall run the entire length of the wall,
- Established on the side of the wall that will be unscaffolded,
- Restricted to entry by employees actively engaged in constructing the wall. No other employees shall be permitted to enter the zone,
- Remain in place until the wall is adequately supported to prevent overturning and to prevent collapse; where the height of a wall is more than 8 feet (2.4 meters), the limited access zone shall remain in place until the requirements of paragraph (b) of this section have been met. **1926.706(a)(1) through (5)**

All masonry walls more than 8 feet (2.4384 meters) in height shall be adequately braced to prevent overturning and to prevent collapse unless the wall is adequately supported so that it will not overturn or collapse. The bracing shall remain in place until permanent supporting elements of the structure are in place. **1926.706(b)**

Confined Spaces

All employees required to enter into confined or enclosed spaces must be instructed as to the nature of the hazards involved, the necessary precautions to be taken, and in the use of required protective and emergency equipment. The employer shall comply with any specific regulations that apply to work in dangerous or potentially dangerous areas. Confined or enclosed spaces include, but are not limited to, storage tanks, process vessels, bins, boilers, ventilation or exhaust ducts, sewers, underground utility vaults, tunnels, pipelines, and open top spaces more than 4 feet deep (1.2 meters) such as pits, tubs, vaults, and vessels. **1926.21(b)(6)(i) through (ii)**

Cranes and Derricks

Before assembly or use of a crane, ground conditions must be firm, drained, and graded so that the equipment manufacturer's specifications for adequate support and degree of level are met. **1926.1402(b)**

A competent person must begin a visual inspection prior to each shift during which the equipment will be used, which must be completed before or during the shift. The inspection must consist of observation for apparent deficiencies. **1926.1412(d)(1)**

A qualified person must conduct a comprehensive inspection at least every 12 months. **1926.1412(f)(1)**

The employer must comply with all manufacturer procedures applicable to the operational functions of equipment, including its use with attachments. **1926.1417(a)**

Hand signal charts must be either posted on the equipment or conspicuously posted in the vicinity of the hoisting operations. **1926.1422**

A personal fall arrest system is permitted to be anchored to the crane/derrick's hook (or other part of the load line) where a qualified person has determined the set-up and rated capacity of the crane/derrick (including the hook, load line, and rigging) meets or exceeds the requirements in §1926.502(d)(15) and no load is suspended from the load line when the personal fall arrest system is anchored to the crane/derrick's hook (or other part of the load line). The equipment operator must be at the work site and know the equipment is being used for this purpose. **1926.1423(j)**

Where available, hoisting routes that minimize the exposure of employees to hoisted loads must be used, to the extent consistent with public safety. **1926.1425(a)**

The employer must ensure that, prior to operating any equipment covered under Subpart CC, the person operating the equipment is qualified or certified to operate the equipment. Exceptions: operation of derricks, sideboom cranes, and equipment with a rated hoisting/lifting capacity of 2,000 pounds or less. **1926.1427(a)(1) through (3)**

On equipment with a rated hoisting/lifting capacity of 2,000 pounds or less the employer must train each operator, prior to operating the equipment, on the safe operation of the type of equipment the operator will be using. **1926.1441(e)**

Demolition

Prior to permitting employees to start demolition operations, a competent person shall make an engineering survey of the structure to determine the condition of the framing, floors, and walls, and possibility of unplanned collapse of any portion of the structure. A similar survey of any adjacent structure where employees may be exposed shall be completed. The employer shall have in writing evidence that such a survey has been performed. **1926.850(a)**

During balling or claiming operations, employers shall not permit any workers in any area that can be adversely affected by demolition operations. Only those workers necessary for the performance of the operations shall be permitted in this area at any other time. **1926.859(a)**

Disposal Chutes

Whenever materials are dropped more than 20 feet (6 meters) to any exterior point of a building, an enclosed chute shall be used. **1926.252(a)**

When debris is dropped through holes in the floor without the use of chutes, the area where the material is dropped shall be enclosed with barricades not less than 42 inches high (106.7 centimeters) and not less than 6 feet (1.8 meters) back from the projected edges of the opening above. Warning signs of the hazard of falling material shall be posted at each level. **1926.252(b)**

Note: During demolition, **1926.852** applies to chutes and **1926.853** applies to the removal of materials through floor openings.

Diving

The employer shall develop and maintain a safe practice manual, and make it available at the dive location for each dive team member. **1910.420(a) made applicable to construction by 1926.1080**

The employer shall keep a record of each dive. The record shall contain the diver's name, his or her supervisor's name, date, time, location, type of dive (scuba, mixed gas, surface supply), underwater and surface conditions, and maximum depth and bottom time. 1**910.423(d)(1)(i) through (vi) made applicable to construction by 1926.1083**

Each dive team member shall have the experience or training necessary to perform assigned tasks safely. **1910.410(a)(1) made applicable to construction by 1926.1076**

Each dive team member shall be briefed on the tasks, safety procedures, unusual hazards or environmental conditions, and modifications made to the operating procedures. **1910.421(f) made applicable to construction by 1926.1081**

The dive shall be terminated when a diver requests it, the diver fails to respond correctly, communication is lost, or when the diver begins to use the reserve breathing gas. **1910.422(i)(1)**

through (4) made applicable to construction by
1926.1082.

Drinking Water

An adequate supply of potable water shall be provided in all places of employment. **1926.51(a)(1)**

Portable drinking water containers shall be capable of being tightly closed and equipped with a tap. **1926.51(a)(2)**

Using a common drinking cup is prohibited. **1926.51(a)(4)**

Where single service cups (to be used but once) are supplied, both a sanitary container for unused cups and a receptacle for used cups shall be provided. **1926.51(a)(5)**

Electrical Installations

Employers must provide either ground-fault circuit interrupters (GFCIs) or an assured equipment grounding conductor program to protect employees from ground-fault hazards at construction sites. The two options are detailed below.

- All 120-volt, single-phase, 15- and 20-ampere receptacles that are not part of the permanent wiring must be protected by GFCIs. Receptacles on smaller generators are exempt under certain conditions, or

- An assured equipment grounding conductor program covering extension cords, receptacles, and cord- and plug-connected equipment must be implemented. The program must include the following:

- A written description of the program,

- At least one competent person to implement the program,

- Daily visual inspections of extension cords and cord- and plug-connected equipment for defects. Equipment found damaged or defective shall not be used until repaired,

- Continuity tests of the equipment grounding conductors or receptacles, extension cords, and cord- and plug-connected equipment. These tests must generally be made every 3 months,
- Equipment that does not meet the above requirements may not be used,
- Required tests shall be recorded. **1926.404(b)(1) (i) through (iii)(e)**

Light bulbs for general illumination must be protected from breakage, and metal shell sockets must be grounded. **1926.405(a)(2)(ii)(E)**

Temporary lights must not be suspended by their cords, unless they are so designed. **1926.405(a)(2) (ii)(F)**

Portable lighting used in wet or conductive locations, such as drums, tanks, and vessels, must be operated at no more than 12 volts or must be protected by a ground-fault circuit interrupter (GFCI). **1926.405(a)(2)(ii)(G)**

Extension cords must be of the three-wire type. Extension cords and flexible cords used with temporary and portable lights must be designed for hard or extra hard usage (for example, types S, ST, and SO). **1926.405(a)(2)(ii)(J)**

Flexible cords must be connected to devices and fittings so that strain relief is provided which will prevent pull from being directly transmitted to joints or terminal screws. **1926.405(g)(2)(iv)**

Listed, labeled, or certified equipment shall be installed and used in accordance with instructions included in the listing, labeling, or certification. **1926.403(b)(2)**

Electrical Work Practices

Employers must not allow employees to work near live parts of electrical circuits, unless the employees are protected by one of the following means:

- Deenergizing and grounding the parts,
- Guarding the part by insulation,

- Any other effective means. **1926.416(a)(1)**

In work areas where the exact location of underground electrical power lines is unknown, employees using jack hammers, bars, or other hand tools that may contact the lines must be protected by insulating gloves. **1926.416(a)(2)**

Barriers or other means of guarding must be used to ensure that workspace for electrical equipment will not be used as a passageway during periods when energized parts of equipment are exposed. **1926.416(b)(1)**

Work spaces, walkways, and similar locations shall be kept clear of cords. **1926.416(b)(2)**

Worn or frayed electric cords or cables shall not be used. **1926.416(e)(1)**

Extension cords shall not be fastened with staples, hung from nails, or suspended by wire. **1926.416(e)(2)**

Equipment or circuits that are deenergized must be rendered inoperative and must have tags attached at all points where the equipment or circuits could be energized. **1926.417(b)**

Excavating and Trenching

The estimated location of utility installations – such as sewer, telephone, fuel, electric, water lines, or any other underground installations that reasonably may be expected to be encountered during excavation work – shall be determined prior to opening an excavation. **1926.651(b)(1)**

Utility companies or owners shall be contacted within established or customary local response times, advised of the proposed work, and asked to establish the location of the utility underground installations prior to the start of actual excavation. When utility companies or owners cannot respond to a request to locate underground utility installations within 24 hours (unless a longer period is required by state or local law), or cannot establish the exact location of these installations, the employer may proceed, provided the employer does so with caution, and provided detection equipment or other acceptable means to locate utility installations are used. **1926.651(b)(2)**

When excavation operations approach the estimated location of underground installations, the exact location of the installations shall be determined by safe and acceptable means. While the excavation is open, underground installations shall be protected, supported, or removed, as necessary, to safeguard employees. **1926.651(b)(3) through (4)**

Each employee in an excavation shall be protected from cave-ins by an adequate protective system except when excavations are made entirely in stable rock, or excavations are less than 5 feet (1.5 meters) in depth and examination of the ground by a competent person provides no indication of a potential cave-in. **1926.652(a)(1)(i) through (ii)**

Protective systems shall have the capacity to resist, without failure, all loads that are intended or could reasonably be expected to be applied or transmitted to the system. **1926.652(a)(2)**

Employees shall be protected from excavated or other materials or equipment that could pose a hazard by falling or rolling into excavations. Protection shall be provided by placing and keeping such materials or equipment at least 2 feet (0.6 meters) from the edge of excavations, or by the use of retaining devices that are sufficient to prevent materials or equipment from falling or rolling into excavations, or by a combination of both if necessary. **1926.651(j)(2)**

Daily inspections of excavations, the adjacent areas, and protective systems shall be made by a competent person for evidence of a situation that could result in possible cave-ins, indications of failure of protective systems, hazardous atmospheres, or other hazardous conditions. An inspection shall be conducted by the competent person prior to the start of work and as needed throughout the shift. Inspections shall also be made after every rainstorm or other hazard increasing occurrence. These inspections are only required when employee exposure can be reasonably anticipated. **1926.651(k)(1)**

Where a competent person finds evidence of a situation that could result in a possible cave-in, indications of failure of protective systems, hazardous atmospheres, or other hazardous conditions, exposed employees shall be removed from the hazardous area until the necessary precautions have been taken to ensure their safety. **1926.651(k)(2)**

A stairway, ladder, ramp, or other safe means of egress shall be located in trench excavations that are 4 feet (1.2 meters) or more in depth so as to require no more than 25 feet (7.6 meters) of lateral travel for employees. **1926.651(c)(2)**

Each employee at the edge of an excavation 6 feet deep (1.8 meters) or more in depth shall be protected from falling by guardrail systems, fences, barricades when the excavations are not readily seen because of plant growth or other visual barrier. **1926.501(b)(7)(i)**

Exits

Exits must be free of all obstructions so they can be used immediately in case of fire or emergency. **1926.34(c)**

Explosives and Blasting

Only authorized and qualified persons shall be permitted to handle and use explosives. **1926.900(a)**

Explosives and related materials shall be stored in approved facilities required under the applicable provisions of the Bureau of Alcohol, Tobacco and Firearms regulations contained in 27 CFR Part 55, Commerce in Explosives. (See Subpart K.) **1926.904(a)**

Smoking and open flames shall not be permitted within 50 feet (15.2 meters) of explosives and detonator storage magazines. **1926.904(c)** Procedures that permit safe and efficient loading shall be established before loading is started. **1926.905(a)**

Eye and Face Protection

Eye and face protection shall be provided when machines or operations present potential for eye or face injury. **1926.102(a)(1)**

Eye and face protective equipment shall meet the requirements of ANSI Z87.1-1968, *Practice for Occupational and Educational Eye and Face Protection.* **1926.102(a)(2)**

Employees involved in welding operations shall be furnished with filter lenses or plates of at least the proper shade number as indicated in Table E-2. **1926.102(b)(1)**

Table E-2 – Filter Lens Shade Numbers for Protection Against Radiant Energy – 1926.102(b)(1)

Welding operation	Shade Number
Shielded metal-arc welding 1/16-, 3/32-, 1/8, 5/32-inch diameter electrodes	10
Gas-shielded arc welding (nonferrous) 1/16, 3/32-, 1/8-, 5/32-inch diameter electrodes	11
Gas-shielded arc welding (nonferrous) 1/16, 3/32-, 1/8-, 5/32-inch diameter electrodes	12
Shielded metal-arc welding 3/16-, 7/32-, 1/4-inch diameter electrodes	12
5/16-, 3/8-inch diameter electrodes	14
Atomic hydrogen welding	10-14
Carbon-arc welding	14
Soldering	2
Torch brazing	3 or 4
Medium cutting, 1 inch to 6 inches	4 or 5
Heavy cutting, over 6 inches	5 or 6
Gas welding (light), up to 1/8-inch	4 or 5
Gas welding (medium), 1/8- to 1/2-inch	5 or 6
Gas welding (heavy), over 1/2-inch	6 or 8

Employees exposed to laser beams shall be furnished suitable laser safety goggles that will protect for the specific wave length of the laser and the optical density adequate for the energy involved. **1926.102(b)(2)(i)**

Fall Protection

Employers are required to assess the workplace to determine if the walking/working surface on which employees are to work have the strength and structural integrity to safely support workers. Employees are not permitted to work on those surfaces until it has been determined that the surfaces have the requisite strength and structural integrity to support the workers. **1926.501(a)(2)**

Where employees are exposed to falling 6 feet (1.8 meters) or more from an unprotected side or edge, the employer must select either a guardrail system, safety net system, or personal fall arrest system to protect the worker. **1926.501(b)(1)**

A personal fall arrest system consists of an anchorage, connectors, body harness and may include a lanyard, deceleration device, lifeline, or a suitable combination of these. Body belts used for fall arrests are prohibited. 1**926.500(b) and 1926.502(d)**

Each employee in a hoist area shall be protected from falling 6 feet (1.8 meters) or more by guardrail systems or personal fall arrest systems. If guardrail systems (or chain gate or guardrail) or portions thereof must be removed to facilitate hoisting operations, as during the landing of materials, and a worker must lean through the access opening or out over the edge of the access opening to receive or guide equipment and materials, that employee must be protected by a personal fall arrest system. **1926.501(b)(3)**

Each employee on walking/working surfaces shall be protected from falling through holes (including skylights) more than 6 feet (1.8 m) above lower levels, by personal fall arrest systems, covers, or guardrail systems erected around such holes. **1926.501(b)(4)(i)**

Each employee on ramps, runways, and other walkways shall be protected from falling 6 feet or more to lower levels by guardrail systems. **1926.501(b)(6)**

Each employee at the edge of an excavation 6 feet deep (1.8 meters) or more in depth shall be protected from falling by guardrail systems, fences, barricades when the excavations are not readily seen because of a visual barrier. **1926.501(b)(7)(i)**

Each employee at the edge of a well, pit, shaft, and similar excavation 6 feet (1.8 meters) or more in depth shall be protected from falling by guardrail systems, fences, barricades, or covers. **1926.501(b)(7)(ii)**

Each employee performing overhand bricklaying and related work 6 feet (1.8 meters) or more above lower levels, on surfaces other than scaffolds, shall be protected by guardrail systems, safety net systems, or personal fall arrest systems, or shall work in a controlled access zone. All employees reaching more than 10 inches (25.4 centimeters) below the level of a walking/working surface on which they are working shall be protected by a guardrail system, safety net system, or personal fall arrest systems. **1926.501(b)(9)**

Each employee engaged in roofing activities on low-slope roofs with unprotected sides and edges 6 feet (1.8 meters) or more above lower levels shall be protected from falling by guardrail, safety net, or personal fall arrest systems or a combination of a:

- Warning line system and guardrail system,
- Warning line system and safety net system,
- Warning line system and personal fall arrest system, or
- Warning line system and safety monitoring system.
- On low-slope roofs 50 feet (15.2 meters) or less in width, the use of a safety monitoring system without a warning line system is permitted. **1926.501(b)(10)**

Each employee on a steep roof with unprotected sides and edges 6 feet (1.8 meters) or more above lower levels shall be protected by guardrail systems with toeboards, safety net systems, or personal fall arrest systems. **1926.501(b)(11)**

Fall Protection, Falling Objects

When an employee is exposed to falling objects, the employer must ensure that each employee wear a hard hat and erect toeboards, screens, or guardrail systems; or erect a canopy structure and keep potential fall objects far enough from the edge of the higher level; or barricade the area to which objects could fall. **1926.501(c)(1) and (2)**

Fall Protection, Wall Openings

Each employee working on, at, above, or near wall openings (including those with chutes attached) where the outside bottom edge of the wall opening is 6 feet (1.8 meters) or more above lower levels and the inside bottom edge of the wall opening is less than 39 inches (1 meter) above the walking/working surface must be protected from falling by the use of a guardrail system, a safety net system, or a personal fall arrest system. **1926.501(b)(14)**

Fire Protection

A fire protection program is to be followed throughout all phases of the construction and demolition work involved. It shall provide for effective firefighting equipment to be available without delay, and designed to effectively meet all fire hazards as they occur. **1926.150(a)(1)**

Firefighting equipment shall be conspicuously located and readily accessible at all times, be periodically inspected, and be maintained in operating condition. **1926.150(a)(2) to (4)**

A fire extinguisher, rated not less than 2A (acceptable substitutes are a 1/2-inch diameter garden-type hose not to exceed 100 feet capable of discharging a minimum of 5 gallons per minute or a 55-gallon drum of water with two fire pails), shall be provided for each 3,000 square feet (270 square meters) of the protected building area, or major fraction thereof. Travel distance from any point of the protected area to the nearest fire extinguisher shall not exceed 100 feet (30.5 meters). **1926.150(c)(1)(i) to (iii)**

The employer shall establish an alarm system at the worksite so that employees and the local fire department can be alerted for an emergency. **1926.150(e)(1)**

Flaggers

High-visibility clothing

For daytime work, the flagger's vest, shirt, or jacket shall be orange, yellow, strong yellow-green or fluorescent versions of these colors. For nighttime work, similar outside garments shall be retroreflective. The retroreflective material shall be orange, yellow, white, silver, strong yellow-green, or a fluorescent version of one of these colors and shall be visible at a minimum distance of 1,000 feet. The retroreflective clothing shall be designed to identify clearly the wearer as a person and be visible through the full range of body motions. *Part VI of the Manual on Uniform Traffic Control Devices* **made applicable to construction by 1926.201(a) and 1926.200(g)(2)**

Hand-signaling procedures

The STOP/SLOW paddle, which gives drivers more positive guidance than red flags, should be the primary hand-signaling device. Flag use should be limited to emergencies and at low-speed and/or low-volume locations that can best be controlled by a single flagger.

The following methods of signaling with STOP/ SLOW paddles should be used:

- To Stop Traffic – The flagger shall face traffic and extend the STOP sign paddle in a stationary position with the arm extended horizontally away from the body. The free arm should be raised with the palm toward approaching traffic.

- To Direct Stopped Traffic to Proceed – The flagger shall face traffic with the SLOW paddle held in a stationary position with the arm extended horizontally away from the body. The flagger should motion with the free hand for traffic to proceed.
- To Alert or Slow Traffic – The flagger shall face traffic with the SLOW sign paddle held in a stationary position with the arm extended horizontally away from the body. The flagger may motion up and down with the free hand, palm down, indicating that the vehicle should slow down.

The following methods of signaling with a flag should be used:

- To Stop Traffic – The flagger shall face traffic and extend the flag staff horizontally across the traffic lane in a stationary position, so that the full area of the flag is visible hanging below the staff. The free arm should be raised with the palm toward approaching traffic.
- To Direct Stopped Traffic to Proceed – The flagger shall face traffic with the flag and arm lowered from view of the driver. With the free hand, the flagger should motion traffic to proceed. Flags shall not be used to signal traffic to proceed.
- To Alert or Slow Traffic – The flagger shall face traffic and slowly wave the flag in a sweeping motion of the extended arm from shoulder level to straight down, without raising the arm above a horizontal position.

Flammable and Combustible Liquids

Only approved containers and portable tanks shall be used for storing and handling flammable and combustible liquids. **1926.152(a)(1)**

No more than 25 gallons (94.7 liters) of flammable or combustible liquids shall be stored in a room outside of an approved storage cabinet. No more than three storage cabinets may be located in a single storage area. **1926.152(b)(1) and (3)**

Inside storage rooms for flammable and combustible liquids shall be of fire-resistant construction, have self-closing fire doors at all openings, 4-inch (10 centimeter) sills or depressed floors, a ventilation system that provides at least six air changes within the room per hour, and electrical wiring and equipment approved for Class 1, Division 1 locations. **1926.152(b)(4)**

Storage in containers outside buildings shall not exceed 1,100 gallons (4,169 liters) in any one pile or area. The storage area shall be graded to divert possible spills away from buildings or other exposures, or shall be surrounded by a curb or dike. **1926.152(c)(1) and (3)**

Outdoor portable tanks shall be located at least 20 feet (6 meters) from any building. **1926.152(c)(4)(i)**

Storage areas shall be free from weeds, debris, and other combustible materials not necessary to the storage. **1926.152(c)(5)**

Flammable liquids shall be kept in closed containers when not actually in use. **1926.152(f)(1)**

Conspicuous and legible signs prohibiting smoking shall be posted in service and refueling areas. **1926.152(g)(9)**

Forklifts (See Powered Industrial Trucks)

Gases, Vapors, Fumes, Dusts, and Mists

Exposure to toxic gases, vapors, fumes, dusts, and mists at a concentration above those specified in Appendix A, shall be avoided. **1926.55(a) and 1926.55 Appendix A**

Administrative or engineering controls must be implemented whenever feasible to comply with Threshold Limit Values. When engineering and administrative controls are not feasible to achieve full compliance, protective equipment or other protective measures shall be used to keep the exposure of employees to air contaminants within the limits prescribed. Any equipment and technical measures used for this purpose must first be approved for each particular use by a competent industrial hygienist or other technically qualified person. Whenever respirators are used, their use shall comply with 1910.134, made applicable to construction by **1926.103. 1926.55(b)**

General Duty Clause

Hazardous conditions or practices not covered in an OSHA standard may be covered under Section 5(a)(1) of the *Occupational Safety and Health Act of 1970*, which states: "Each employer shall furnish to each of his employees employment and a place of employment which are free from recognized hazards that are causing or are likely to cause death or serious physical harm to his employees."

Grinding

All abrasive wheel bench and stand grinders shall be equipped with safety guards that cover the spindle ends, nut and flange projections, and are strong enough to withstand the effects of a bursting wheel. **1926.303(b)(1), (2), and (c)(1)**

An adjustable work rest of rigid construction shall be used on floor and bench-mounted grinders, with the work rest kept adjusted to a clearance not to exceed 1/8-inch (0.3 centimeters) between the work rest and the surface of the wheel. **1926.303(c)(2)**

All abrasive wheels shall be closely inspected and ring-tested before mounting to ensure that they are free from cracks or other defects. **1926.303(c)(7)**

Portable abrasive wheel tools used for external grinding shall be provided with safety guards, except when the wheels are 2 inches (5 centimeters) or less in diameter or the work location makes it impossible (then a wheel equipped with safety flanges shall be used). **1926.303(c)(3)**

Portable abrasive wheel tools used for internal grinding shall be provided with safety flanges, except when the wheels are 2 inches (5 centimeters) or less in diameter or the wheel is entirely inside the work. **1926.303(c)(4)**

Hand Tools

All hand and power tools and similar equipment, whether furnished by the employer or employee, shall be maintained in a safe condition. Employers shall not issue or permit the use of unsafe hand tools. **1926.300(a) and 1926.301(a)**

Wrenches shall not be used when jaws are sprung to the point that slippage occurs. Impact tools shall be kept free of mushroomed heads. The wooden handles of tools shall be kept free of splinters or cracks and shall be kept tight in the tool. **1926.301(b) through (d)**

Electric power operated tools shall either be approved double-insulated, or be properly grounded in accordance with Subpart K of the standard. **1926.302(a)(1)**

Hazard Communication

Employers shall develop, implement, and maintain at the workplace a written hazard communication program for their workplaces. Employers must inform their employees of the availability of the program, including the required list(s) of hazardous chemicals, and material safety data sheets required. **1910.1200(e)(1) and (e)(4) made applicable to construction by 1926.59**

The chemical manufacturer, importer, or distributor shall ensure that each container of hazardous chemicals leaving the workplace is labeled, tagged, or marked with the identity of the hazardous chemical(s), the appropriate hazard warnings, and the name and address of the chemical manufacturer, importer, or other responsible party. **1910.1200(f)(1) made applicable to construction by 1926.59**

The employer shall ensure that each container of hazardous chemicals in the workplace is labeled, tagged or marked with the following information:

- Identity of the hazardous chemical(s) contained therein, and
- Appropriate hazard warnings, or alternatively, words, pictures, symbols, or combination thereof, which provide at least general information regarding the hazards of the chemicals, and which, in conjunction with the other information immediately available to employees under the hazard communication program, will provide employees with specific information regarding the physical and health hazards of the hazardous chemical. **1910.1200(f)(5) made applicable to construction by 1926.59**

Chemical manufacturers and importers shall obtain or develop a material safety data sheet for each hazardous chemical they produce or import. Employers shall have a material safety data sheet for each hazardous chemical they use. **1910.1200(g)(1) made applicable to construction by 1926.59**

Employers shall provide employees with information and training on hazardous chemicals in their work area at the time of their initial assignment, and whenever a new hazard is introduced into their work area. Employers shall also provide employees with information on any operations in their work area where hazardous chemicals are present, and the location and availability of the written hazard communication program, including the required list(s) of hazardous chemicals, and material safety data sheets required by the standard. **1910.1200(h)(1) and (2)(i) through (iii) made applicable to construction by 1926.59**

Employers who produce, use, or store hazardous chemicals at multi-employer workplaces shall additionally ensure that their hazard communication program includes the methods the employer will use to provide other employer(s) with a copy of the material safety data sheet for hazardous chemicals which employees of other employer(s) may be exposed to while working; the methods the employer will use to inform other employer(s) of any precautionary measures for the protection of employees; and the methods the employer will use to inform the other employer(s) of the labeling system used in the workplace. **1910.1200(e)(2) made applicable to construction by 1926.59**

Hazardous Waste Operations

Employers must develop and implement a written safety and health program for employees involved in hazardous waste operations. At a minimum, the program shall have an organizational structure, a comprehensive workplan, standard operating procedures, a site specific safety and health plan (which need not repeat the standard operating procedures), the training program, and medical surveillance program. **1926.65(b)(1)**

A site control program also shall be developed and shall include, at a minimum, a map, work zones, buddy systems, site communications – including alerting means for emergencies – standard operating procedures or safe work practices, and identification of the nearest medical assistance. **1926.65(d)(3)**

Training must be provided for all site employees, their supervisors, and management who are exposed to health or safety hazards before they are permitted to engage in hazardous waste operations. **1926.65(e)(1)(i)**

Head Protection

Head protective equipment (helmets) shall be worn in areas where there is a possible danger of head injuries from impact, flying or falling objects, or electrical shock and burns. **1926.100(a)**

Helmets for protection against impact and penetration of falling and flying objects shall meet the requirements of ANSI Z89.1-1969. Helmets for protection against electrical shock and burns shall meet the requirements of ANSI Z89.2-1971. **1926.100(b) and (c)**

Hearing Protection

Feasible engineering or administrative controls shall be utilized to protect employees against sound levels in excess of those shown in **Table D-2.**

When engineering or administrative controls fail to reduce sound levels within the limits of Table D-2, ear protective devices shall be provided and used. **1926.52(b) and .101(a)**

Plain cotton is not an acceptable protective device. **1926.101(c)**

In all cases where the sound levels exceed the values shown in Table D-2, a continuing, effective hearing conservation program shall be administered. **1926.52(d)(1)**

OSHA considers the following topics to be valuable in a hearing conservation program:

- Monitoring employee noise exposures (to determine if sound levels exceed those shown in **1926.52 Table D-2**),
- Using engineering, work practice and administrative controls, and personal protective equipment measures (see "Training and Hazard Control" **1926.21(b)(2)**),
- Fitting each overexposed employee with appropriate hearing protectors **1926.101(b)**,
- Training employees in the effects of noise and protection measures (see "Training and Hazard Control" **1926.21(b)(2)**,
- Explaining procedures for preventing further hearing loss, and recordkeeping and reporting.

For more information: OSHA describes hearing conservation program requirements for general industry in the General Industry Occupational Noise Exposure standard **1910.95(c) – (o)**.

Table D-2 – Permissible Noise Exposures – 1926.52(d)(1)

Duration per day, hours:	Sound Level/dBA slow response
8	90
6	92
4	95
3	97
2	100
1 ½	102
1	105
1/2	110
1/4 or Less	115

Exposure to impulsive or impact noise should not exceed 140 dB peak sound pressure level. **1926.52(e)**

Heating Devices, Temporary

When heating devices are used, fresh air shall be supplied in sufficient quantities to maintain the health and safety of workers. **1926.154(a)(1)**

Solid fuel salamanders are prohibited in buildings and on scaffolds. **1926.154(d)**

Highway Work Zones (See Flaggers and Signs, Signals, and Barricades)

Hoists, Material and Personnel

The employer shall comply with the manufacturer's specifications and limitations. **1926.552(a)(1)**

Rated load capacities, recommended operating speeds, and special hazard warnings or instructions shall be posted on cars and platforms. **1926.552(a)(2)**

Hoistway entrances of material hoists shall be protected by substantial full width gates or bars that are painted with diagonal contrasting colors such as black and yellow stripes. **1926.552(b)(2)**

Hoistway doors or gates of personnel hoists shall be not less than 6 feet 6 inches (198.1 meters) high and shall be protected with mechanical locks that cannot be operated from the landing side and that are accessible only to persons on the car. **1926.552(c)(4)**

Overhead protective coverings shall be provided on the top of the hoist cage or platform. **1926.552(b)(3) and (c)(7)**

All material hoists shall conform to the requirements of ANSI A10.5-1969, *Safety Requirements for Material Hoists*. **1926.552(b)(8)**

The requirements of 1926.1431 apply when one or more employees are hoisted using equipment covered by Subpart CC, Cranes and Derricks in Construction.

Hooks (See Wire Ropes, Chains, and Ropes)

Housekeeping

Form and scrap lumber with protruding nails and all other debris shall be kept clear from all work areas. **1926.25(a)**

Combustible scrap and debris shall be removed at regular intervals. **1926.25(b)**

Containers shall be provided for collection and separation of all refuse. Covers shall be provided on containers used for flammable or harmful substances. Waste shall be disposed of at frequent intervals. **1926.25(c)**

Illumination

Construction areas, aisles, stairs, ramps, runways, corridors, offices, shops, and storage areas shall be lighted to not less than the minimum illumination intensities listed in Table D-3 while any work is in progress. **1926.26**

Table D-3 – Minimum Illumination Intensities in Footcandles

Footcandles: Area of Operation
5..........General construction area lighting
3..........General construction areas, concrete placement, excavation, waste areas, accessways, active storage areas, loading platforms, refueling, and field maintenance areas
5..........Indoor warehouses, corridors, hallways, and exitways
5..........Tunnels, shafts, and general underground work areas (Exception: minimum of 10 footcandles is required at tunnel and shaft heading during drilling, mucking, and scaling. Bureau of Mines- approved cap lights shall be acceptable for use in the tunnel heading)
10..........General construction plant and shops (e.g., batch plants, screening plants, mechanical and electrical equipment rooms, carpenters shops, rigging lofts and active store rooms, barracks or living quarters, locker or dressing rooms, mess halls, indoor toilets, and workrooms)
30..........First-aid stations, infirmaries, and offices

1926.56(a)

Jointers

A jointer guard shall automatically adjust itself to cover the unused portion of the head and the section of the head on the working side and the back side of the fence or cage. The jointer guard shall remain in contact with the material at all times. **ANSI 01.1-1961, section 4.3.2, incorporated by reference to construction by 1926.304(f)**

Ladders

A ladder (or stairway) must be provided at all work points of access where there is a break in elevation of 19 inches (48.2 centimeters) or more except if a suitable ramp, runway, embankment, or personnel hoist is provided to give safe access to all elevations. **1926.1051(a)**

Portable and fixed ladders with structural defects – such as broken or missing rungs, cleats or steps, broken or split rails, or corroded components – shall be withdrawn from service by immediately tagging "DO NOT USE" or marking in a manner that identifies them as defective, or shall be blocked, such as with a plywood attachment that spans several rungs. Repairs must restore ladder to its original design criteria. **1926.1053(b)(16), (17) (i) through (iii) and (18)**

Portable non-self-supporting ladders shall have clear access at top and bottom and be placed at an angle so the horizontal distance from the top support to the foot of the ladder is approximately one-quarter the working length of the ladder. **1926.1053(b)(5)(i) and (b)(9)**

Portable ladders used for access to an upper landing surface must extend a minimum of 3 feet (0.9 meters) above the landing surface, or where not practical, be provided with grab rails and be secured against movement while in use. **1926.1053(b)(1)**

Ladders must have nonconductive siderails if they are used where the worker or the ladder could contact energized electrical conductors or equipment. **1926.1053(b)(12)**

Job-made ladders shall be constructed for their intended use. Cleats shall be uniformly spaced not less than 10 inches (25.4 centimeters) apart, nor more than 14 inches (35.5 centimeters) apart. **1926.1053(a)(3)(i)**

Wood job-made ladders with spliced side rails must be used at an angle where the horizontal distance is one-eighth the working length of the ladder. **1926.1053(b)(5)(ii)**

Fixed ladders must be used at a pitch no greater than 90 degrees from the horizontal, measured from the back side of the ladder. **1926.1053(b)(5) (iii)**

Ladders must be used only on stable and level surfaces unless secured to prevent accidental movement. **1926.1053(b)(6)**

Ladders must not be used on slippery surfaces unless secured or provided with slip-resistant feet to prevent accidental movement. Slip-resistant feet must not be used as a substitute for the care in placing, lashing, or holding a ladder upon a slippery surface. **1926.1053 (b)(7)**

Employers must provide a training program for each employee using ladders and stairways. The program must enable each employee to recognize hazards related to ladders and stairways and to use proper procedures to minimize these hazards. For example, employers must ensure that each employee is trained by a competent person in the following areas, as applicable:

- The nature of fall hazards in the work area,
- The correct procedures for erecting, maintaining, and disassembling the fall protection systems to be used,
- The proper construction, use, placement, and care in handling of all stairways and ladders, and
- The maximum intended load-carrying capacities of ladders used.

In addition, retraining must be provided for each employee, as necessary, so that the employee maintains the understanding and knowledge acquired through compliance with the standard. **1926.1060(a) and (b)**

Lasers

Only qualified and trained employees shall be assigned to install, adjust, and operate laser equipment. **1926.54(a)**

Employees shall wear proper (antilaser) eye protection when working in areas where there is a potential exposure to direct or reflected laser light greater than 0.005 watts (5 milliwatts). **1926.54(c)**

Beam shutters or caps shall be utilized, or the laser turned off, when laser transmission is not actually required. When the laser is left unattended for a substantial period of time – such as during lunch hour, overnight, or at change of shifts – the laser shall be turned off. **1926.54(e)**

Employees shall not be exposed to light intensities in excess of the following: direct staring – 1 microwatt per square centimeter, incidental observing – 1 milliwatt per square centimeter, and diffused reflected light – 2 1/2 watts per square centimeter. **1926.54(j)(1) through (3)**

Employees shall not be exposed to microwave power densities in excess of 10 milliwatts per square centimeter. **1926.54(1)**

Lead

Each employer who has a workplace or operation covered by this standard shall initially determine if any employee may be exposed to lead at or above the action level of 30 micrograms per cubic meter (30 µg/m3) of air calculated as an 8-hour time-weighted average. **1926.62(d)(1)(i)**

The employer shall assure that no employee is exposed to lead at concentrations greater than 50 micrograms per cubic meter (50 µg/m3) of air averaged over an 8-hour period (the permissible exposure limit PEL). **1926.62(c)(1)**

Whenever there has been a change of equipment, process, control, personnel, or a new task has been initiated that may result in additional employees being exposed to lead at or above the action level or may result in employees already exposed at or above the action level being exposed above the PEL, the employer shall conduct additional monitoring. **1926.62(d)(7)**

Training shall be provided in accordance with the Hazard Communication standard and additional training shall be provided for employees exposed at or above the action level. **1926.62(1)**

Prior to the start of the job, each employer shall establish and implement a written compliance program. **1926.62(e)(2)(i)**

Where employees are required to use respirators, the employer must implement a respiratory protection program. **1910.134(b) through (d) (except (d)(iii)), and (f) through (m) made applicable to construction by 1926.62(f)(2)(i)**

Where airborne concentrations of lead equal or exceed the action level at any time, an initial medical examination consisting of blood sampling and analysis shall be made available for each employee prior to initial assignment to the area. **1926.62 Appendix B, viii, paragraph (j)**

Lift Slab

Lift-slab operations shall be designed and planned by a registered professional engineer who has experience in lift-slab construction. Such plans and designs shall be implemented by the employer and shall include detailed instructions and sketches indicating the prescribed method of erection. **1926.705(a)**

Jacking equipment shall be capable of supporting at least two and one-half times the load being lifted during jacking operations. Also, do not overload the jacking equipment. **1926.705(d)**

During erection, no employee, except those essential to the jacking operation, shall be permitted in the building or structure while jacking operations are taking place unless the building or structure has been reinforced sufficiently to ensure its integrity. **1926.705(k)(1)**

Equipment shall be designed and installed to prevent slippage; otherwise, the employer shall institute other measures, such as locking or blocking devices, which will provide positive connection between the lifting rods and attachments and will prevent components from disengaging during lifting operations. **1926.705(p)**

Liquefied Petroleum Gas

Each system shall have containers, valves, connectors, manifold valve assemblies, and regulators of an approved type. **1926.153(a)(1)**

Every container and vaporizer shall be provided with one or more approved safety relief valves or devices. **1926.153(d)(1)**

Containers shall be placed upright on firm foundations or otherwise firmly secured. **1926.153(g) and (h)(11)**

Portable heaters shall be equipped with an approved automatic device to shut off the flow of gas in the event of flame failure. **1926.153(h)(8)**

All cylinder connectors shall be equipped with an excess flow valve to minimize the flow of gas in the event the fuel line becomes ruptured. **1926.153(i)(2)**

Storage of liquefied petroleum gas within buildings is prohibited. **1926.153(j)**

Storage locations shall have at least one approved portable fire extinguisher rated not less than 20-B:C. **1926.153(l)**

Medical Services and First Aid

The employer shall ensure the availability of medical personnel for advice and consultation on matters of occupational health. **1926.50(a)**

When a medical facility is not reasonably accessible for the treatment of injured employees, a person qualified to render first aid shall be available at the worksite. **1926.50(c)**

First-aid supplies when required should be readily available. **1926.50(d)(1)**

In areas where 911 is not available, the telephone numbers of the physicians, hospitals, or ambulances shall be conspicuously posted. **1926.50(f)**

Motor Vehicles and Mechanized Equipment

All vehicles in use shall be checked at the beginning of each shift to ensure that all parts, equipment, and accessories that affect safe operation are in proper operating condition and free from defects. All defects shall be corrected before the vehicle is placed in service. **1926.601 (b)(14)**

No employer shall use any motor vehicle, earthmoving, or compacting equipment having an obstructed view to the rear unless:

▪ The vehicle has a reverse signal alarm distinguishable from the surrounding noise level, or the vehicle is backed up only when an observer signals that it is safe to do so. **1926.601(b)(4)(i) through (ii) and 602(a)(9)(i) through (ii)**

Heavy machinery, equipment, or parts thereof that are suspended or held aloft shall be substantially blocked to prevent falling or shifting before employees are permitted to work under or between them. **1926.600(a)(3)(i)**

Noise (See Hearing Protection)

Personal Protective Equipment

The employer is responsible for requiring the wearing of appropriate personal protective equipment in all operations where there is an exposure to hazardous conditions or where the need is indicated for using such equipment to reduce the hazard to the employees. **1926.28(a) and 1926.95(a) through (c)**

Employers must provide most personal protective equipment at no cost to employees. **1926.95(d)(1), see 1926.95(d)(2) through (6) for exceptions**

OSHA requires employers to provide and for employees to use specific types of personal protective equipment in specific standards throughout 29 CFR 1926. These standards include, but are not limited to:

- Foot protection. **1926.96**
- Head protection. **1926.100**
- Hearing protection. **1926.101**
- Eye and face protection. **1926.102**
- Respiratory protection. **1910.134 made applicable to construction by 1926.103**
- Safety belts, lifelines, and lanyards. **1926.104**
- Safety nets. **1926.105**
- Working over or near water (life jackets). **1926.106**
- Personal fall arrest system. **1926.502(d)**
- Protective equipment for use during electrical work. **1926.416 and 1926.951**

Head, hearing, eye and face, safety nets, fall protection, and working over or near water are covered in detail in this digest.

Powder-Actuated Tools

Only trained employees shall be allowed to operate powder-actuated tools. **1926.302(e)(1)**

All powder-actuated tools shall be tested daily before use and all defects discovered before or during use shall be corrected. **1926.302(e)(2) through (3)**

Tools shall not be loaded until immediately before use. Loaded tools shall not be left unattended. **1926.302(e)(5) through (6)**

Power Transmission and Distribution

Existing conditions shall be determined before starting work, by an inspection or a test. Such conditions shall include, but not be limited to, energized lines and equipment, condition of poles, and the location of circuits and equipment including power and communications, cable television, and fire-alarm circuits. **1926.950(b)(1)**

Electric equipment and lines shall be considered energized until determined otherwise by testing or until grounding. **1926.950(b)(2) and .954(a)**

Operating voltage of equipment and lines shall be determined before working on or near energized parts. **1926.950(b)(3)**

Rubber protective equipment shall comply with the provisions of the ANSI J6 series, and shall be visually inspected before use. **1926.951(a)(1)(i) through (ii)**

Protective equipment of material other than rubber shall provide equal or better electrical and mechanical protection. **1926.951(a)(iv)**

Powered Industrial Trucks (Forklifts)

Each powered industrial truck operator must be competent to operate a powered industrial truck safely, as demonstrated by the successful completion of the training and evaluation. **1910.178(l)(1)(i) made applicable to construction by 1926.602(d)**

Training shall consist of a combination of formal instruction (e.g., lecture, discussion, interactive computer learning, video tape, written material), practical training (demonstrations performed by the trainer and practical exercises performed by the trainee), and evaluation of the operator's performance in the workplace. **1910.178(l)(2)(ii) made applicable to construction by 1926.602(d)**

Power Transmission, Mechanical

Belts, gears, shafts, pulleys, sprockets, spindles, drums, flywheels, chains, or other reciprocating, rotating, or moving parts of equipment shall be guarded if such parts are exposed to contact by employees or otherwise constitute a hazard. Guarding shall meet the requirement of ANSI B15.1-1953 (R 1958), Safety Code for Mechanical Power Transmission Apparatus. **1926.300(b)(2)**

Process Safety Management of Highly Hazardous Chemicals

Employers shall develop a written plan of action regarding employee participation and consult with employees and their representatives on the conduct and development of process hazards analyses and on the development of the other elements of process safety management. **1926.64(c)(1) through (2)**

The employer, when selecting a contractor, shall obtain and evaluate information regarding the contract employer's safety performance and programs. **1926.64(h)(2)(i)**

The contract employer shall assure that each contract employee is trained in the work practices necessary to safely perform his/her job. **1926.64(h)(3)(i)**

The employer shall perform a pre-startup safety review for new facilities and for modified facilities when the modification is significant enough to require a change in the process safety information. **1926.64(i)(1)**

The employer shall establish and implement written procedures to maintain the ongoing integrity of process equipment. **1926.64(j)(2)**

Radiation, Ionizing

Pertinent provisions of the Nuclear Regulatory Commission (NRC) Standards for Protection Against Radiation (10 CFR Part 20) relating to protection against occupational radiation exposure shall apply. **1926.53(a)**

Any activity that involves the use of radioactive materials or X-rays, whether or not under license from the Nuclear Regulatory Commission, shall be performed by competent persons specially trained in the proper and safe operation of such equipment. **1926.53(b)**

Railings

Top edge height of top rails or equivalent guardrail system members shall have a vertical height of approximately 42 inches (106.6 centimeters), plus or minus 3 inches (7.6 centimeters) above the walking/working level. **1926.502(b)(1)**

Guardrail systems shall be surfaced so as to prevent injury to an employee, with a strength to withstand at least 200 pounds (90 kilograms), the minimum requirement applied in any outward or downward direction, at any point along the top edge. **1926.502(b)(3) and (6)**

A stair railing shall be of construction similar to a standard railing with a vertical height of not less than 36 inches (91.5 centimeters) from the upper surface of top rail to the surface of tread in line with face of riser at forward edge of tread. **1926.1052(c)(3)(i)**

Recordkeeping: Recording and Reporting Requirements

Within 8 hours after the death of any employee or report of the inpatient hospitalization of three or more employees, as the result of a work-related incident, you must report this to the closest OSHA office, or call (800) 321-6742. **1904.39(a) and (b)(7)**

If your company had more than 10 employees at any time during the last calendar year, you must keep the OSHA injury and illness records using the OSHA Forms 300, 300-A, and 301 or the equivalent form. **1904.1(a)(2) and 1904.29(a) and (b)(4)**

If your company had 10 or fewer employees at all times during the last calendar year, you do not need to keep OSHA injury and illness records unless OSHA or the Bureau of Labor Statistics informs you in writing that you must keep these records. **1904.1(a)(1)**

Each recordable injury or illness must be entered on the OSHA Forms 300 and 301 within 7 days of receiving the information. **1904.29(b)(3)**

OSHA injury and illness records must be kept for all projects. If the project is 1 year or longer a separate OSHA 300 log must be kept. If the projects are less than 1 year, these projects may be placed on one OSHA 300 log that covers all short-term projects. These records may be kept at a central location as long as the information is transferred within 7 days. **1904.30(a), (b)(1) and (2)**

The OSHA 300 log must be verified, certified by a company executive, and posted at the end of each calendar year. The log must be posted no later than February 1 of the following year and remain posted until April 30. **1904.32 (a) and (b)**

The OSHA 300 and 301 logs must be kept for 5 years following the year to which they relate. **1904.33(a) and 1904.44**

Reinforced Steel

All protruding reinforced steel, onto and into which employees could fall, shall be guarded to eliminate the hazard of impalement. **1926.701(b)**

No employee (except those essential to the post-tensioning operations) shall be permitted to be behind the jack during tensioning operations. **1926.701(c)(1)**

Reinforcing steel for walls, piers, columns, and similar vertical structures shall be adequately supported to prevent overturning and to prevent collapse. **1926.703(d)(1)**

Employers shall take measures to prevent unrolled wire mesh from recoiling. Such measures may include, but are not limited to, securing each end of the roll or turning over the roll. **1926.703(d)(2)**

Respiratory Protection

In emergencies, or when feasible engineering or administrative controls are not effective in controlling toxic substances, appropriate respiratory protective equipment shall be provided by the employer and shall be used.

1910.134(a)(1) made applicable to construction by 1926.103

Employers must select a NIOSH-certified respirator. The respirator must be used in compliance with the conditions of its certification. **1910.134(d)(1)(ii) made applicable to construction by 1926.103**

Respiratory protective devices shall be appropriate for the hazardous material involved and the extent and nature of the work requirements and conditions. **1910.134(d)(1)(i) made applicable to construction by 1926.103**

Employees required to use respiratory protective devices shall be thoroughly trained in their use. **1910.134(k) made applicable to construction by 1926.103**

Respiratory protective equipment shall be inspected regularly and maintained in good condition. **1910.134(h) made applicable to construction by 1926.103**

Rollover Protective Structures (ROPS)

Rollover protective structures (ROPS) apply to the following types of materials handling equipment: all rubber-tired, self-propelled scrapers, rubber-tired frontend loaders, rubber-tired dozers, wheel-type agricultural and industrial tractors, crawler tractors, crawler-type loaders, and motor graders, with or without attachments, that are used in construction work. This requirement does not apply to sideboom pipelaying tractors. **1926.1000(a)(1)**

Safety Nets

Safety nets must be installed as close as practicable under the walking/working surface on which employees are working, but in no case more than 30 feet (9.14 meters) below such level. When nets are used on bridges, the potential fall area from the walking/working surface to the net shall be unobstructed. **1926.502(c)(1)**

Safety nets and their installations must be capable of absorbing an impact force equal to that produced by the drop test. **1926.502(c)(4)**

Saws

Band Saws

All portions of band saw blades shall be enclosed or guarded, except for the working portion of the blade between the bottom of the guide rolls and the table. **ANSI 01.1-1961, incorporated by reference to construction by 1926.304(f)**

Band saw wheels shall be fully encased. **ANSI 01.1-1961, incorporated by reference to construction by 1926.304(f)**

Portable Circular Saws

Portable, power-driven circular saws shall be equipped with guards above and below the base plate or shoe. The lower guard shall cover the saw to the depth of the teeth, except for the minimum arc required to allow proper retraction and contact with the work, and shall automatically return to the covering position when the blade is removed from the work. **1926.304(d)**

Circular saws shall have a constant pressure switch that will shut off the power when the pressure is released. **1926.300(d)(3)**

Radial Saws

Radial saws shall have an upper guard that completely encloses the upper half of the saw blade. The sides of the lower exposed portion of the blade shall be guarded by a device that will automatically adjust to the thickness of and remain in contact with the material being cut. **1926.304(g)(1)**

Radial saws used for ripping shall have nonkickback fingers or dogs. **ANSI 01.1-1961, incorporated by reference to construction by 1926.304(f)**

Radial saws shall be installed so that the cutting head will return to the starting position when released by the operator. **ANSI 01.1-1961, incorporated by reference to construction by 1926.304(f)**

Swing or Sliding Cut-Off Saws

All swing or sliding cut-off saws shall be provided with a hood that will completely enclose the upper half of the saw. **ANSI 01.1-1961, incorporated by reference to construction by 1926.304(f)**

Limit stops shall be provided to prevent swing or sliding type cut-off saws from extending beyond the front or back edges of the table. **ANSI 01.1-1961, incorporated by reference to construction by 1926.304(f)**

Each swing or sliding cut-off saw shall be provided with an effective device to return the saw automatically to the back of the table when released at any point of its travel. **ANSI 01.1-1961, incorporated by reference to construction by 1926.304(f)**

Inverted sawing of sliding cut-off saws shall be provided with a hood that will cover the part of the saw that protrudes above the top of the table or material being cut. **ANSI 01.1-1961, incorporated by reference to construction by 1926.304(f)**

Table Saws

Circular table saws shall have a hood over the portion of the saw above the table, so mounted that the hood will automatically adjust itself to the thickness of and remain in contact with the material being cut. **1926.304(h)(1)**

Circular table saws shall have a spreader aligned with the blade, spaced no more than 1/2-inch (1.27-centimeters) behind the largest blade mounted in the saw. This provision does not apply when grooving, dadoing, or rabbiting. **ANSI 01.1-1961, incorporated by reference to construction by 1926.304(f)**

Circular table saws used for ripping shall have nonkickback fingers or dogs. **ANSI 01.1-1961, incorporated by reference to construction by 1926.304(f)**

Feeder attachments shall have the feed rolls or other moving parts covered or guarded so as to protect the operator from hazardous points. **1926.304(c)**

Scaffolds, General Requirements

Scaffolds shall be erected, moved, dismantled, or altered only under the supervision and direction of a competent person. **1926.451(f)(7)**

Scaffolds are any temporary elevated platform (supported or suspended) and its supporting structure (including points of anchorage), used for supporting employees or materials or both. **1926.450(b)**

Each employee who performs work on a scaffold shall be trained by a person qualified to recognize the hazards associated with the type of scaffold used and to understand the procedures to control or minimize those hazards. The training shall include such topics as the nature of any electrical hazards, fall hazards, falling object hazards, the maintenance and disassembly of the fall protection systems, the use of the scaffold, handling of materials, the capacity and the maximum intended load. **1926.454(a)**

Fall protection (guardrail systems and personal fall arrest systems) must be provided for each employee on a scaffold more than 10 feet (3.1 meters) above a lower level. **1926.451(g)(1)**

Each scaffold and scaffold component shall support without failure its own weight and at least 4 times the maximum intended load applied or transmitted to it. Suspension ropes and connecting hardware must support 6 times the intended load. Scaffolds and scaffold components shall not be loaded in excess of their maximum intended loads or rated capacities, whichever is less. **1926.451(a)(1), (a)(4), (f)(1)**

The scaffold platform shall be planked or decked as fully as possible. **1926.451(b)(1)**

The platform shall not deflect more than 1/60 of the span when loaded. **1926.451(f)(16)**

The work area for each scaffold platform and walkway shall be at least 18 inches (46 centimeters) wide. When the work area must be less than 18 inches (46 centimeters) wide, guardrails and/or personal fall arrest systems shall still be used. **1926.451(b)(2)(ii)**

Access must be provided when the scaffold platforms are more than 2 feet (0.6 m) above or below a point of access. Direct access is acceptable when the scaffold is not more than 14 inches (36 centimeters) horizontally and not more than 24 inches (61 centimeters) vertically from the other surfaces. Crossbraces shall not be used as a means of access. **1926.451(e)(1) and (e)(8)**

A competent person shall inspect the scaffold, scaffold components, and ropes on suspended scaffolds before each work shift and after any occurrence which could affect the structural integrity and authorize prompt corrective action. **1926.450 (b), 451(f)(3)**

Scaffold, Bricklaying

Employees doing overhand bricklaying from a supported scaffold shall be protected by a guardrail or personal fall arrest system on all sides except the side where the work is being done. **1926.451(g)(1)(vi)**

Scaffold, Erectors and Dismantlers

A competent person shall determine the feasibility for safe access and fall protection for employees erecting and dismantling supported scaffolds. **1926.451(e)(9) and (g)(2)**

Scaffold, Fall Arrest Systems

A personal fall arrest system consists of an anchorage, connectors, a body harness, a lanyard, and may include a deceleration device. Anchorages used for attachment shall be capable of supporting at least 5,000 pounds (22.2 kN) per employee attached or shall be designed, installed, and used under the supervision of a qualified person as part of a complete personal fall arrest system which maintains a safety factor of at least two. Personal fall arrest systems used on scaffolds must be attached by lanyard to a vertical lifeline, horizontal lifeline, or scaffold structural member. **1926.502(d)(15) and 1926.451(g)(3)**

Vertical or horizontal lifelines may be used. **1926.451(g)(3)(ii) through (iv)**

Lifelines shall be independent of support lines and suspension ropes and not attached to the same anchorage point as the support or suspension ropes. **1926.451(g)(3)(iii) and (iv)**

Employees must be tied off when working from an aerial lift. Fall restraint systems or personal fall arrest systems may be used. The use of personal fall arrest systems must comply with Subpart M. **1926.453(b)(2)(v) and 1926.502(d)**

Scaffold, Guardrails

Guardrails shall be installed along all open sides and ends of platforms before the scaffold is released for use by employees other than the erection and dismantling crews. Guardrails are not required on the front edge of a platform if the front edge of the platform is less than 14 inches (36 centimeters) from the face of the work. For plastering and lathing, the distance is 18 inches (46 centimeters) or less from the front edge. When outrigger scaffolds are attached to supported scaffolds the distance is 3 inches (8 centimeters) or less from the front edge of the outrigger. **1926.451(b)(3) and (g)(4)**

The toprail for scaffolds must be 38 inches (0.97 meters) to 45 inches (1.2 meters) from the platform. Midrails are to be installed approximately halfway between the toprail and the platform surface. **1926.451(g)(4)(ii) and (iii)**

Toeboards or other barriers are to be used to protect employees working below. **1926.451(h)**

When screens and mesh are used for guardrails, they shall extend from the top edge of the guardrail system to the scaffold platform, and along the entire opening between the supports. **1926.451(g)(4)(v)**

Crossbracing is not acceptable as an entire guardrail system but is acceptable for a toprail when the crossing point of the two braces is between 38 inches (0.9 meters) and 48 inches (1.3 meters) above the work platform and for midrails when between 20 inches (0.5 meters) and 30 inches (0.8 meters) above the work platform. The end points of the crossbracing shall be no more than 48 inches (1.3 meters) apart vertically. **1926.451(g)(4)(xv)**

Scaffolds, Mobile

Scaffolds shall be braced by cross, horizontal, or diagonal braces, or a combination thereof. Scaffolds must be plumb, level, and squared. All brace connections must be secured. **1926.452(w)(1)**

Each employee on a scaffold more than 10 feet above a lower level shall be protected from falling to that lower level by use of guardrail systems or personal fall arrest systems. **1926.451(g)(1), (g)(1) (vii), and (g)(4)**

Scaffold, Planking

Scaffold planking shall be capable of supporting without failure its own weight and at least 4 times the intended load. Solid sawn wood, fabricated planks, and fabricated platforms may be used as scaffold planks, following the recommendations by the manufacturer or a lumber grading association or inspection agency. Tables showing maximum permissible spans, rated load capacity, nominal thickness, etc., are in Appendix A of Subpart L (1)(b) and (c). **1926.451(a)(1)**

Scaffolds, Supported

Supported scaffolds are platforms supported by legs, outrigger beams, brackets, poles, uprights, posts, frames, or similar rigid support. The structural members, poles, legs, posts, frames, and uprights, shall be plumb and braced to prevent swaying and displacement. **1926.451(b) and (c)(3)**

Supported scaffolds poles, legs, posts, frames, and uprights shall bear on base plates and mud sills, or on another adequate firm foundation. **1926.451(c)(2)**

Either the manufacturer's recommendation or the following placements shall be used for guys, ties, and braces: install guys, ties, and braces at the closest horizontal member to the 4:1 height and repeat vertically with the top restraint no further than the 4:1 height from the top:

Vertically

Every 20 feet (6.1 meters) or less for scaffolds less than 3 feet (0.9 meters) wide;

Every 26 feet (7.9 meters) or less for scaffolds more than 3 feet (0.9 meters) wide;

Horizontally

At each end;

At intervals not to exceed 30 feet (9.1 meters) from one end. **1926.451(c)(1)(ii)**

Scaffolds, Suspension (Swing)

Each employee more than 10 feet (3.1 meters) above a lower level shall be protected from falling by guardrails and a personal fall arrest system when working from single or two-point suspended scaffolds and self-contained adjustable scaffolds that are supported by ropes. **1926.451(g) (1)(ii) and (iv)**

Each employee 10 feet (3.1 meters) above a lower level shall be protected from falling by a personal fall arrest system when working from a boatswain's chair, ladder jack, needle beam, float, or catenary scaffolds. **1926.451(g)(1)(i)**

Lifelines shall be independent of support lines and suspension ropes and not attached to the same anchorage point as the support or suspension ropes. **1926.451(g)(3)(iii) and (iv)**

A competent person shall inspect the ropes for defects prior to each workshift and after every occurrence which could affect a rope's integrity, evaluate the direct connections that support the load, and determine if two-point and multi-point scaffolds are secured from swaying. **1926.451(d)(3)(i), (d)(10), (d)(18), (f)(3)**

The use of repaired wire rope is prohibited. **1926.451(d)(7)**

Tiebacks shall be secured to a structurally sound anchorage on the building or structure. **1926.451(d)(3)(ix)**

Tiebacks shall not be secured to standpipes, vents, other piping systems, or electrical conduit. **1926.451(d)(3)(ix) and (d)(5)**

A single tieback shall be installed perpendicular to the face of the building or structure. Two tiebacks installed at opposing angles are required when a perpendicular tieback cannot be installed. **1926.451(d)(3)(x)**

Only those items specifically designed as counterweights shall be used. Sand, gravel, masonry units, rolls of roofing felt, and other such materials shall not be used as counterweights. **1926.451(d)(3)(ii) and (iii)**

Counterweights used for suspended scaffolds shall be made of materials that can not be easily dislocated. **1926.451(d)(3)(ii)**

Counterweights shall be secured by mechanical means to the outrigger beams. **1926.451(d)(3)(iv)**

Signs, Signals, and Barricades (See Flaggers)

Construction areas shall be posted with legible traffic signs at points of hazard. **1926.200 (g)(1)**

Barricades for protection of employees shall conform to Part 6 of the *Manual on Uniform Traffic Control Devices*. **1926.202**

Silica

Appropriate engineering controls, personal protective equipment, respirators, and work practices shall be used to protect employees from crystalline silica. **1926.55(a) and (b) and OSHA National Emphasis Program on Crystalline Silica 1/24/2008**

Stairs

A stairway or ladder must be provided at all worker points of access where there is a break in elevation of 19 inches (48.3 centimeters) or more and no ramp, runway, sloped embankment, or personnel hoist is provided. **1926.1051(a)**

Except during construction of the actual stairway, skeleton metal frame structures and steps must not be used (where treads and/or landings are to be installed at a later date), unless the stairs are fitted with secured temporary treads and landings. **1926.1052(b)(2)**

When there is only one point of access between levels, it must be kept clear to permit free passage by workers. If free passage becomes restricted, a second point of access must be provided and used. **1926.1051(a)(3)**

When there are more than two points of access between levels, at least one point of access must be kept clear. **1926.1051(a)(4)**

All stairway and ladder fall protection systems must be provided and installed as required by the stairway and ladder rules before employees begin work that requires them to use stairways or ladders and their respective fall protection systems. **1926.1051(b)**

Stairways that will not be a permanent part of the structure on which construction work is performed must have landings at least 30 inches deep and 22 inches wide (76.2 x 55.9 centimeters) at every 12 feet (3.6 meters) or less of vertical rise. **1926.1052(a)(1)**

Stairways must be installed at least 30 degrees, and no more than 50 degrees, from the horizontal. **1926.1052(a)(2)**

Where doors or gates open directly onto a stairway, a platform must be provided, and the swing of the door shall not reduce the effective width of the platform to less than 20 inches (50.8 centimeters). **1926.1052(a)(4)**

Except during construction of the actual stairway, stairways with metal pan landings and treads must not be used where the treads and/or landings have not been filled in with concrete or other material, unless the pans of the stairs and/or landings are temporarily filled in with wood or other material. All treads and landings must be replaced when worn below the top edge of the pan. **1926.1052(b)(1)**

Stairways having four or more risers, or rising more than 30 inches in height (76.2 centimeters), whichever is less, must have at least one handrail. A stairrail also must be installed along each unprotected side or edge. **1926.1052(c)(1)(i) through (ii)**

Midrails, screens, mesh, intermediate vertical members, or equivalent intermediate structural members must be provided between the top rail and stairway steps of the stairrail system. **1926.1052(c)(4)**

Midrails, when used, must be located midway between the top of the stairrail system and the stairway steps. **1926.1052(c)(4)(i)**

The height of handrails must not be more than 37 inches (93.9 centimeters) nor less than 30 inches (76.2 centimeters) from the upper surface of the handrail to the surface of the tread in line with face of riser at forward edge of tread. **1926.1052(c)(6)**

When the top edge of a stairrail system also serves as a handrail, the height of the top edge must not be more than 37 inches (94 cm) nor less than 36 inches (91.5 cm) from the upper surface of the stairrail system to the surface of the tread, in line with face of riser at forward edge of the tread. **1926.1052(c)(7)**

Temporary handrails must have a minimum clearance of 3 inches (7.6 centimeters) between the handrail and walls, stairrail systems, and other objects. **1926.1052(c)(11)**

Unprotected sides and edges of stairway landings must be provided with guardrail systems. **1926.1052(c)(12)**

Steel Erection

Each employee engaged in a steel erection activity who is on a walking/working surface with an unprotected side or edge more than 15 feet (4.6 meters) above a lower level shall be protected from fall hazards by guardrail systems, safety net systems, personal fall arrest systems, positioning device systems or fall restraint systems. **1926.760(a)(1)**

Connectors more than two stories or 30 feet (9.1 meters) above a lower level, whichever is less, shall be protected by guardrail systems, safety net systems, personal fall arrest systems, positioning devices systems, or fall restraint systems. **1926.760(b)(1)**

Connectors at heights over 15 feet and up to 30 feet above a lower level shall be provided with a personal fall arrest system, positioning device system, or fall restraint system and wear the equipment necessary to be tied off; or be provided with other means of protection from fall hazards in accordance with **1926.760(a)(1). 1926.760(b)(3)**

Training shall be provided for all employees exposed to fall hazards. Special training shall be provided to connectors, workers in controlled decking zones, and those rigging for multiple lifts. **1926.761(c)**

Steel erection begins when written notification that the concrete in the footings, piers, and walls or the mortar in the masonry piers and walls has attained the strength to support the loads imposed during steel erection. **1926.752(b)**

Shear connectors (such as headed steel studs, steel bars or steel lugs), reinforcing bars, deformed anchors or threaded studs shall not be attached to the top flanges of beams, joists or beam attachments so that they project vertically from or horizontally across the top flange of the member until after the metal decking, or other walking/working surface, has been installed. **1926.754(c)(1)**

Columns shall be anchored by a minimum of four anchor rods (anchor bolts). **1926.755(a)(1)**

Solid web structural members shall be secured with at least two bolts per connection before being released from the hoisting line. **1926.756(a)(1)**

Open web joists must be field bolted at each end of the bottom chord before being released from the hoisting line. **1926.757(a)(1)(iii)**

Decking shall be laid tightly and secured. **1926.754(e)(5)**

Controlled decking zones shall be clearly marked and access limited to only those employees engaged in leading edge work. **1926.760(c)(2) and (3)**

Cranes used in steel erection shall be inspected prior to each shift by a competent person. Routes for suspended loads shall be planned to ensure no employee is required to work directly under the load except for connecting or hooking or unhooking. Hooks with self-closing latches shall be used. All loads shall be rigged by a qualified rigger. Multiple lifts shall hoist a maximum of five members. **1926.753(c)(1)(i), (d)(1) and (e)(1)(ii)**

Storage

All materials stored in tiers shall be secured to prevent sliding, falling, or collapsing. **1926.250(a)(1)**

Aisles and passageways shall be kept clear and in good repair. **1926.250(a)(3)**

Storage of materials shall not obstruct exits. **1926.151(d)(1)**

Materials shall be stored with due regard to their fire characteristics. **1926.151(d)(2)**

Tire Cages

A safety tire rack, cage, or equivalent protection shall be provided and used when inflating, mounting, or dismounting tires installed on split rims, or rims equipped with locking rings or similar devices. **1926.600(a)(2)**

Toeboards

Toeboards, when used to protect workers from falling objects, shall be erected along the edge of the overhead walking/working surface. **1926.502(j)(1)**

Toeboards shall be capable of withstanding, without failure, a force of at least 50 pounds (222 N) applied in any downward or outward direction at any point along the toeboard. **1926.502(j)(2)**

A standard toeboard shall be at least 3 1/2 inches (9 centimeters) in height and may be of any substantial material either solid or open, with openings not to exceed 1 inch (2.54 centimeters) in greatest dimension. **1926.502(j)(3)**

Toilets

Toilets shall be provided according to the following: 20 or fewer persons – one facility; 20 or more persons – one toilet seat and one urinal per 40 persons; 200 or more persons – one toilet seat and one urinal per 50 workers. **1926.51(c)(1)**

This requirement does not apply to mobile crews having transportation readily available to nearby toilet facilities. **1926.51(c)(4)**

Training and Inspections

The employer shall initiate and maintain such programs as may be necessary to provide for frequent and regular inspections of the job site, materials, and equipment by designated competent persons. **1926.20(b)(1) through (2)**

The employer should avail himself of the safety and health training programs the Secretary provides. **1926.21(b)(1)**

The employer shall instruct each employee in the recognition and avoidance of unsafe conditions and in the regulations applicable to his work environment to control or eliminate any hazards or other exposure to illness or injury. **1926.21(b)(2)**

The use of any machinery, tool, material, or equipment that is not in compliance with any applicable requirement of Part 1926 is prohibited. **1926.20(b)(3)**

The employer shall permit only those employees qualified by training or experience to operate equipment and machinery. **1926.20(b)(4)**

Underground Construction

The employer shall provide and maintain safe means of access and egress to all work stations. **1926.800(b)(1)**

The employer shall control access to all openings to prevent unauthorized entry underground. Unused chutes, manways, or other openings shall be tightly covered, bulkheaded, or fenced off, and shall be posted with signs indicating "Keep Out" or similar language. Complete or unused sections of the underground facility shall be barricaded. **1926.800(b)(3)**

Unless underground facilities are sufficiently completed so that the permanent environmental controls are effective and the remaining construction activity will not cause any environmental hazard or structural failure within the facilities, the employer shall maintain a check-in/check-out procedure that will ensure that aboveground designated personnel can determine an accurate count of the number of persons underground in the event of an emergency. **1926.800(c)**

All employees shall be instructed to recognize and avoid hazards associated with underground construction activities. **1926.800(d)**

Hazardous classifications are for "potentially gassy" and "gassy" operations. **1926.800(h)** The employer shall assign a competent person to perform all air monitoring to determine proper ventilation and quantitative measurements of potentially hazardous gases. **1926.800(j)(1)(i)(A)**

Fresh air shall be supplied to all underground work areas in sufficient quantities to prevent dangerous or harmful accumulation of dust, fumes, mists, vapors, or gases. **1926.800(k)(1)(i)**

Washing Facilities

The employer shall provide adequate washing facilities for employees engaged in operations involving harmful substances. Washing facilities shall be near the worksite and shall be so equipped as to enable employees to remove all harmful substances. **1926.51(f)**

Water, Working Over or Near

Employees working over or near water, where the danger of drowning exists, shall be provided with U.S. Coast Guard-approved life jackets or buoyant work vests. **1926.106(a)**

Welding, Cutting, and Heating

Employers shall instruct employees in the safe use of welding equipment. **1926.350(d) and 1926.351(d)**

Proper precautions (isolating welding and cutting, removing fire hazards from the vicinity, providing a fire watch) for fire prevention shall be taken in areas where welding or other "hot work" is being done. No welding, cutting, or heating shall be done where the application of flammable paints, or the presence of other flammable compounds or heavy dust concentrations creates a fire hazard. **1926.352(a) through (c) & (f)**

Arc welding and cutting operations shall be shielded by noncombustible or flameproof screens to protect employees and other persons in the vicinity from direct arc rays. **1926.351(e)**

When electrode holders are to be left unattended, the electrodes shall be removed and the holder shall be placed or protected so that they cannot make electrical contact with employees or conducting objects. **1926.351(d)(1)**

All arc welding and cutting cables shall be completely insulated and be capable of handling the maximum current requirements for the job. There shall be no repairs or splices within 10 feet (3 meters) of the electrode holder, except where splices are insulated equal to the insulation of the cable. Defective cable shall be repaired or replaced. **1926.351(b)(1) through (2) and (4)**

Employees performing such operations in the open air shall be protected by filter-type respirators in accordance with the requirements of 1910.134, except that employees performing such operations on beryllium-containing base or filler metals shall be protected with air line respirators in accordance with 1910.134. **1926.353(c)(3)**

Fuel gas and oxygen hose shall be easily distinguishable and shall not be interchangeable. Hoses shall be inspected at the beginning of each shift and shall be repaired or replaced if defective. **1926.350(f)(1) and (3)**

General mechanical ventilation, local exhaust ventilation, air line respirators, and other protection shall be provided, as required, when welding, cutting or heating:

- Zinc, lead, cadmium, chromium, mercury, or materials bearing, based, or coated with beryllium in enclosed spaces,
- Stainless steel with inert-gas equipment,
- In confined spaces, and
- Where an unusual condition can cause an unsafe accumulation of contaminants. **1926.353(b)(1), (c)(1)(i) through (iv), (c)(2)(i) through (iv), (d)(1) (iv), and (e)(1)**

Proper eye protective equipment to prevent exposure of personnel shall be provided. **1926.353(e)(2)**

Wire Ropes, Chains, and Ropes

Wire ropes, chains, ropes, and other rigging equipment shall be inspected prior to use and as necessary during use to ensure their safety. Defective gear shall be removed from service. **1926.251(a)(1)**

Job or shop hooks and links or makeshift fasteners formed from bolts, rods, or other such attachments shall not be used. **1926.251(b)(3)**

When U-bolts are used for eye splices, the U-bolt shall be applied so that the "U" section is in contact with the dead end of the rope. **1926.251(c) (5)(i)**

When U-bolt wire rope clips are used to form eyes, the following table shall be used to determine the number and spacing of clips. **1926.251(c)(5)**

Table H-2 – Number and Spacing of U-Bolt Wire Rope Clips – 1926.251(c)(5)

Improved plow steel, rope diameter (inches)	Number of clips Drop forged	Number of clips Other material	Minimum spacing (inches)
1/2 (1.27 cm)	3	4	3 (7.62 cm)
5/8 (.625 cm)	3	4	3-3/4 (8.37 cm)
3/4 (.75 cm)	4	5	4-1/2 (11.43 cm)
7/8 (.875 cm)	4	5	5-1/4 (12.95 cm)
1 (2.54 cm)	5	6	6 (15.24 cm)
1-1/8 (2.665 cm)	6	6	6-3/4 (15.99 cm)
1-1/4 (2.79 cm)	6	7	7-1/2 (19.05 cm)
1-3/8 (2.915 cm)	7	7	8-1/4 (20.57 cm)
1-1/2 (3.81 cm)	7	8	9 (22.86 cm)

Woodworking Machinery

All fixed power-driven woodworking tools shall be provided with a disconnect switch that can be either locked or tagged in the off position. **1926.304(a)**

All woodworking tools and machinery shall meet applicable requirements of ANSI 01.1-1961, *Safety Code for Woodworking Machinery*. **1926.304(f)**

Complaints, Emergencies and Further Assistance

Workers have the right to a safe workplace. The *Occupational Safety and Health Act of 1970* (OSH Act) was passed to prevent workers from being killed or seriously harmed at work. The law requires employers to provide their employees with working conditions that are free of known dangers. Workers may file a complaint to have OSHA inspect their workplace if they believe that their employer is not following OSHA standards or that there are serious hazards. Further, the Act gives complainants the right to request that their names not be revealed to their employers. It is also against the law for an employer to fire, demote, transfer, or discriminate in any way against a worker for filing a complaint or using other OSHA rights.

To report an emergency, file a complaint, or seek OSHA advice, assistance, or products, call (800) 321-OSHA (6742) or contact your nearest OSHA regional, area, or state plan office listed or linked to at the end of this publication. The teletypewriter (TTY) number is (877) 889-5627. You can also file a complaint online by visiting OSHA's website at www.osha.gov. Most complaints submitted online may be resolved informally over the phone or by fax with your employer. Written complaints, that are signed by a worker or their representative and submitted to the closest OSHA office, are more likely to result in an on-site OSHA inspection.

Compliance Assistance Resources

OSHA can provide extensive help through a variety of programs, including free workplace consultations, compliance assistance, voluntary protection programs, strategic partnerships, alliances, and training and education. For more information on any of the programs listed below, visit OSHA's website at www.osha.gov or call 1-800-321-OSHA (6742).

Establishing an Injury and Illness Prevention Program

The key to a safe and healthful work environment is a comprehensive injury and illness prevention program.

Injury and illness prevention programs, known by a variety of names, are universal interventions that can substantially reduce the number and severity of workplace injuries and alleviate the associated financial burdens on U.S. workplaces. Many states have requirements or voluntary guidelines for workplace injury and illness prevention programs. In addition, numerous employers in the United States already manage safety using injury and illness prevention programs, and we believe that all employers can and should do the same. Employers in the construction industry are already required to have a health and safety program. Most successful injury and illness prevention programs are based on a common set of key elements. These include management leadership, worker participation, hazard identification, hazard prevention and control, education and training, and program evaluation and improvement. Visit OSHA's website at http://www.osha.gov/dsg/topics/safetyhealth/index. html for more information and guidance on establishing effective injury and illness prevention programs in the workplace.

Compliance Assistance Specialists

OSHA has compliance assistance specialists throughout the nation who can provide information to employers and workers about OSHA standards, short educational programs on specific hazards or OSHA rights and responsibilities, and information on additional compliance assistance resources. Contact your local OSHA office for more information.

OSHA Consultation Service for Small Employers

The OSHA Consultation Service provides **free assistance** to small employers to help them identify and correct hazards, and to improve their injury and illness prevention program. Most of these services are delivered on site by state government agencies or universities using well-trained professional staff.

Consultation services are available to private sector employers. Priority is given to small employers with the most hazardous operations or in the most high-hazard industries. These programs are largely funded by OSHA and are delivered at no cost to employers who request help. Consultation services are separate from enforcement activities. To request such services, an employer can phone or write to the OSHA Consultation Program. See the Small Business section of OSHA's website for contact information for the consultation offices in every state.

- **Safety and Health Achievement Recognition Program**
  Under the consultation program, certain exemplary employers may request participation in OSHA's Safety and Health Achievement Recognition Program (SHARP). Eligibility for participation includes, but is not limited to, receiving a full-service, comprehensive consultation visit, correcting all identified hazards, and developing an effective injury and illness prevention program.

Cooperative Programs

OSHA offers cooperative programs to help prevent fatalities, injuries and illnesses in the workplace.

- **OSHA's Alliance Program**
  Through the Alliance Program, OSHA works with groups committed to worker safety and health to prevent workplace fatalities, injuries, and illnesses. These groups include businesses, trade or professional organizations, unions, consulates, faith- and community-based organizations, and educational institutions. OSHA and the groups work together to develop compliance assistance tools and resources, share information with workers and employers, and educate workers and employers about their rights and responsibilities.

- **Challenge Program**
  This program helps employers and workers improve their injury and illness prevention program and implement an effective system to prevent fatalities, injuries and illnesses.

- **OSHA Strategic Partnership Program (OSPP)**
  Partnerships are formalized through tailored agreements designed to encourage, assist and recognize partner efforts to eliminate serious hazards and achieve model workplace safety and health practices.

- **Voluntary Protection Programs (VPP)**
  The VPP recognize employers and workers in private industry and federal agencies who have implemented effective injury and illness prevention programs and maintain injury and illness rates below national Bureau of Labor Statistics averages for their respective industries. In VPP, management, labor, and OSHA work cooperatively and proactively to prevent fatalities, injuries, and illnesses.

OSHA Training Institute Education Centers

The OSHA Training Institute (OTI) Education Centers are a national network of nonprofit organizations authorized by OSHA to conduct occupational safety and health training to private sector workers, supervisors and employers.

Susan Harwood Training and Education Grants

OSHA provides grants to nonprofit organizations to provide worker education and training on serious job hazards and avoidance/prevention strategies.

Information and Publications

OSHA has a variety of educational materials and electronic tools available on its website at www.osha.gov. These include Safety and Health Topics Pages, Safety Fact Sheets, Expert Advisor software, copies of regulations and compliance directives, videos and other information for employers and workers. OSHA's software programs and eTools walk you through safety and health issues and common problems to find the best solutions for your workplace.

OSHA's extensive publications help explain OSHA standards, job hazards, and mitigation strategies and provide assistance in developing effective safety and health programs.

For a listing of free publications, visit OSHA's website at www.osha.gov or call 1-800-321-OSHA (6742).

QuickTakes

OSHA's free, twice-monthly online newsletter, *QuickTakes*, offers the latest news about OSHA initiatives and products to assist employers and workers in finding and preventing workplace hazards. To sign up for *QuickTakes*, visit OSHA's website at www.osha.gov and click on *QuickTakes* at the top of the page.

Contacting OSHA

To order additional copies of this publication, to get a list of other OSHA publications, to ask questions or to get more information, to contact OSHA's free consultation service, or to file a confidential complaint, contact OSHA at 1-800-321-OSHA (6742), (TTY) 1-877-889-5627 or visit www.osha.gov.

**For assistance, contact us.
We are OSHA. We can help.
It's confidential.**

OSHA Regional Offices

Dallas, TX 75202
(972) 850-4145 (972) 850-4149 Fax
(972) 850-4150 FSO Fax

Region VII
Kansas City Regional Office
(IA*, KS, MO, NE)
Two Pershing Square Building
2300 Main Street, Suite 1010
Kansas City, MO 64108-2416
(816) 283-8745 (816) 283-0547 Fax

Region VIII
Denver Regional Office
(CO, MT, ND, SD, UT*, WY*)
1999 Broadway, Suite 1690
Denver, CO 80202
(720) 264-6550 (720) 264-6585 Fax

Region IX
San Francisco Regional Office
(AZ*, CA*, HI*, NV*, and American Samoa,
Guam and the Northern Mariana Islands)
90 7th Street, Suite 18100
San Francisco, CA 94103
(415) 625-2547 (415) 625-2534 Fax

Region X
Seattle Regional Office
(AK*, ID, OR*, WA*)
300 Fifth Avenue, Suite 1280
Seattle, WA 98104
(206) 757-6700 (206) 757-6705 Fax

*These states and territories operate their own OSHA-approved job safety and health plans and cover state and local government employees as well as private sector employees. The Connecticut, Illinois, New Jersey, New York and Virgin Islands programs cover public employees only. (Private sector workers in these states are covered by Federal OSHA). States with approved programs must have standards that are identical to, or at least as effective as, the Federal OSHA standards.

Note: To get contact information for OSHA area offices, OSHA-approved state plans and OSHA consultation projects, please visit us online at www.osha.gov or call us at 1-800-321-OSHA (6742).

OSHA-Approved State Plans

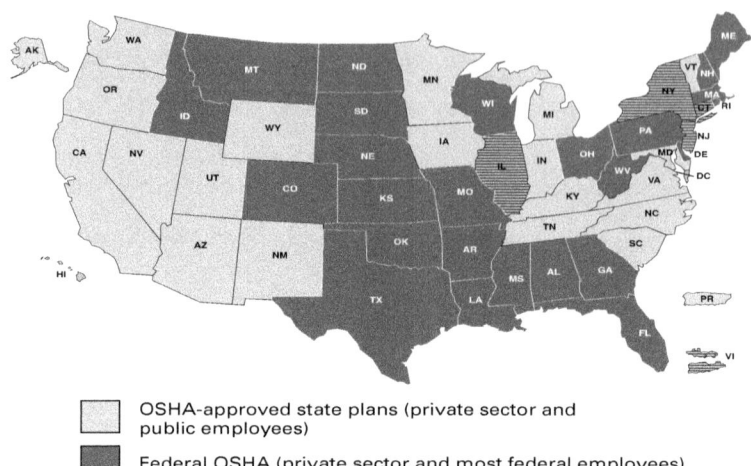

☐ OSHA-approved state plans (private sector and public employees)

■ Federal OSHA (private sector and most federal employees)

▨ OSHA-approved state plans (for public employees only; private sector employees are covered by Federal OSHA)

(800) 321-OSHA (6742)